DOCKSIDE

STAGE **4** BOOK 3

MISSING

Sue Graves

RISING STARS

JJ was cleaning Zigzag's tank.
Zigzag was JJ's pet snake.

But the snake was slipping and sliding out of its tank. It was trying to slide into JJ's bag to find food.

"You need feeding," said JJ.
He went to get some food.

4

But when JJ got back, Zigzag was missing.

"He's never done that before," said Dad.
"Don't worry, we'll find him."

But it wasn't Zigzag. The hissing was coming from a water pipe. The pipe had a hole in it. Water was leaking out.

"Turn off the water fast!" yelled Dad. "The tap is under the kitchen sink."

"You're soaking wet," he said to Dad with a grin, "but don't worry. I'm fast at fixing pipes. You had better stay here to dry off."

The plumber soon came running out looking upset. He was shaking and panting.

"I was thinking what to do first," said the plumber. "Then I saw a s— s— snake. It was slipping and sliding in my toolbox."

"Zigzag!" shouted JJ.

Zigzag was sleeping in the plumber's toolbox.

JJ put Zigzag back into its tank while the plumber went back to fixing the pipe.

"What a day!" said Dad. "We've had leaking pipes and missing snakes ..."

"Yes," said JJ smiling a big smile. "Both of them hissing all day!"